A Personal History:
The Afro-American Texans
STORIES FOR YOUNG READERS

A Personal History:
The Afro-American Texans
STORIES FOR YOUNG READERS

Marian L. Martinello
Writer and Educational Consultant

Melvin M. Sance
Principal Researcher

The University of Texas
Institute of Texan Cultures — San Antonio
1982

STORIES FOR YOUNG READERS

The following books are designed specifically for school-age readers and contain historical fact, interesting information and dynamic accounts of people in Texas history which both entertain and inform:

With Domingo Leal in San Antonio, 1734; Who Are the Chinese Texans?; Our Mexican Ancestors, Volume One; and *A Personal History: The Afro-American Texans.*

The Afro-American Texans
©1982: The University of Texas
   Institute of Texan Cultures—San Antonio

Jack R. Maguire, Executive Director
Pat Maguire, Director of Publications and Programs
Production Staff: Sandra Carr, David Haynes, A.S. Korac,
   Meredith Rees and Tom Shelton

Library of Congress Catalog Card Number 78-57799
International Standard Book Number 0-86701-005-3

First Edition

This publication was made possible, in part, by a grant from the Houston Endowment, Inc.

Printed in the United States of America

TABLE OF CONTENTS

Introduction 7

1528 11
THE SLAVE WHO EXPLORED THE
AMERICAN SOUTHWEST
Esteban

Spanish Texas Grows 17

1820 19
SLAVE AND SETTLER IN
EARLY TEXAS
Kiamata

1835 23
Fighters for
Texas Independence

1836 31
Republic and
Early Statehood

1861 37
CIVIL WAR HERO
Milton M. Holland

1866 43
A TIME OF RECONSTRUCTION
After the Civil War

1877 53
WEST POINT GRADUATE
Henry Flipper

1879 57
Education

1888 *Trail Riders and Cowboys*	*59*
1910 *Sportsmen*	*69*
1910 *Musicians and Performers*	*73*
War Heroes	*81*
Afro-American Folklore	*85*
Political Leaders	*89*
Personal Histories	*95*

Introduction

A person's history is the story of his or her life up to now.

Your history is the story of your life:
Where you came from.
What you have done.
Who you are!
What is your personal history so far?

You can find out by asking yourself questions like those on the Personal History Record (PHR) at the back of this book.

Personal History Records can be made for other people too.

We can ask them for information or find answers to questions about their lives in books or from people who know about them. When a PHR is completed for someone, it tells us something about that person's life history. A whole stack of PHRs gives us information about many people. When those people have something special in common, we can put the information together to write *their* history.

If each of your relatives completed a Personal History Record, you could write a history of your family by putting together all the information you find on the PHRs. This book does that for a group of people who have something in common.

The people in this book would probably consider themselves as the Afro-American race. Yet, many of them in talking to each other would probably call themselves black, at least if they were talking today. Although some have parents or grandparents who were white or Indian, all have African ancestors. Some came to this country with the Spanish explorers as slaves. Most were brought to this country later and sold as slaves to white Americans.

Slavery is a cruel social institution which allows people to force other people to work for them. Slaves were considered to be no more than property, and were, therefore, treated as such.

They were often whipped to keep them from running away. Others who broke the slave laws imposed upon them sometimes were killed.

During American slavery black children were frequently taken from their mothers and sent far away. Fathers too were often sold and separated from their families.

Although blacks were suppressed and denied citizenship during slavery, and prejudices were held against them even after slavery was abolished, blacks made outstanding contributions to their American culture. They acted in ways which brought honor to their race and gained the respect of others.

Many white Americans never approved of the inhumane treatment of slaves. The disagreement between these whites and slave owners was a cause of the Civil War.

Most of the slaves came from Africa. However, much of the African culture was destroyed by two centuries of slavery in the United States. In its place grew the Afro-American culture of today.

All of the people in this book are Americans. And because they have lived in Texas for most of their lives, many of them are also Texans. They are members of that race in Texas which makes up about 12 percent of the state's population. They are the Afro-American Texans.

Each of the people in this book is special. Each has done something with his or her life. Many have suffered great hardships. All have done something to help our nation grow and prosper.

In the pages which follow you will meet Afro-Americans who were or are:

    Explorers
    Pioneers and Frontier People
    Freedom Fighters and Soldiers
    Settlers, Slaves and Freedmen
    Cowhands and Ranchers
    Ministers and Teachers
    Musicians, Actors and Storytellers
    Sportsmen
    Businessmen
    Legislators and Politicians

Because many of the people in this book lived a long time ago, we don't know exactly how they would answer our questions. But we know enough about them to be able to write answers they might have given if we were able to talk with them.

As you read the stories about the Afro-American Texans in this book, you will learn about the personal histories of real people. Then, maybe you will want to complete PHRs for Afro-American Texans you know to add to this book.

1528

THE SLAVE WHO EXPLORED THE AMERICAN SOUTHWEST

Esteban

Esteban, also known as Estevan which means Stephen in English, was the first black man known by name to have come to Texas. He was one of the first discoverers and explorers of the American Southwest.

That was less than 50 years after Columbus reached the American continent! Although he was a slave, Esteban was a leader in his time.

This is his personal history, as much as we know about it and as he would tell it if he were alive today.

Where were you born? I was born in northwest Africa in the 1500's, but I lived many years in America.

Azzemmour, Esteban's birthplace

Which of those places do you think of as home?	There is really no place I call home because I moved around so much. I spent most of my adult life in the American Southwest. I helped discover and explore the places you now call New Mexico, Arizona and Texas.
How did you come to this part of the world?	I came to this country more than 400 years ago with the Narváez expedition. At that time I was the slave of Andrés Dorantes, who was a Spanish explorer. We set out from Spain to explore the coast of the Gulf of Mexico. In 1528 we were shipwrecked near Galveston Island. Only four of us survived: besides me, there was my master, Dorantes, and two Spanish adventurers, Alonso del Castillo and Alvar Nuñez Cabeza de Vaca.
What happened to you and the other survivors?	We were captured by Indians who lived in the place where we were shipwrecked. Life was very hard for us while we were their captives. We did not understand their language, and, since we were not familiar with the country, we could not plan an escape.

Survivors discovered by Karankawa Indians

What did you do? I had a special talent—the ability to learn different languages quickly and easily. I was also a fearless and ambitious man who knew how to survive even in the worst conditions. One of the first things I did was to dress like our Indian captors.

I learned their language and served as a translator for the Indians and the Spaniards. Fortunately, the four of us had some knowledge of medicine—how to use herbs to cure different illnesses. We were able to use that knowledge to heal sick Indians, and we became known as medicine men. The Indians respected us, gave us gifts and allowed us to move from village to village to do our healing. This gave me a chance to discover where trails and villages were located and where food and water could be found.

Is that how you were able to explore the country? Yes. With the information I had gathered Dorantes, Castillo, Cabeza de Vaca and I were able to travel over territory that had never before been explored by Europeans. We spent eight years traveling from the Gulf coast across to the Pacific coast of Mexico.

Where did your journey end? We finally arrived in Mexico City.

Why Mexico City? At that time Mexico was a Spanish colony. The Spanish survivors of the shipwreck who traveled across the American Southwest with my help wanted to tell Antonio de Mendoza, the ruler of Mexico City, about the places we had been and, especially, about the Seven Cities of Gold.

What were the Seven Cities of Gold? They were Indian pueblos which we had heard were made of gold. Probably they just looked like that in the setting sun. But I think we almost

Esteban with Alvar Nuñez Cabeza de Vaca

believed in the gold ourselves. In any event, Mendoza decided to capture the rich cities. I became lead scout of the expedition he sent to conquer the cities for the Spanish crown. An old priest named Marcos de Niza was named head of the expedition, but because of his age and my ability to communicate with the Indians, I, in fact, became head of the expedition.

But weren't you a slave? I belonged to Dorantes, yes. And he sold me to Mendoza after he decided to settle in Mexico.

Technically, I was not a free man. But my talents and experience were recognized by the Spaniards. So it is not surprising that Mendoza would choose me to be an advance scout for a party to find the rich cities.

My instructions were to send back wooden crosses as signals that I had found the treasures. The size of the cross I sent was to tell how important the discovery was. A big cross meant that a very wealthy place had been found.

When I got to a Zuni pueblo, I sent back two crosses. The second one was quite large. I thought it would surely bring the expedition to conquer the city. But I was too excited to wait for the priest, so I went ahead. I commanded the Indians to surrender. In that moment, I was no longer a slave. I was a conqueror!

What did the Indians do? They warned me to retreat.

Did you? No. I stood my ground. I really thought that I could conquer the Zuni city single-handed.

The fact is that I was outnumbered, alone and defenseless when the Zunis attacked me.

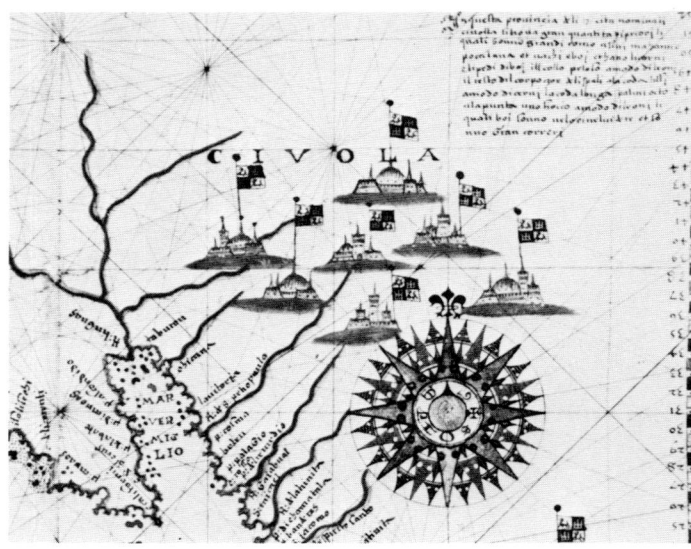

The Seven Cities of Gold on a 1578 map

Esteban was killed by the Zunis' arrows when he tried to enter their pueblo. But stories of his adventures became legends. Other explorers followed him into the American Southwest searching for wealth.

Spanish Texas Grows

Between the time Esteban set foot on American soil and the time when Kiamata lived as a young slave and settler in Texas, almost two centuries had passed.

During that time many Afro-Americans were among the early settlers in Spanish Texas. They lived and worked as free people. The only thing they were not permitted to do was hold positions in government.

They were farmers, merchants, teachers, shoemakers, carpenters, teamsters, ministers, laborers and domestic workers.

Some intermarried with Spanish settlers. All helped Texas grow from a Spanish frontier to an independent republic.

Kiamata and Jane Long at Point Bolivar

1820
SLAVE AND SETTLER IN EARLY TEXAS
Kiamata

While Texas was under Spanish rule, many Afro-Americans were free, with the legal and political rights of Spanish citizenship.

When settlement of the land started, cheap labor was needed to work on the plantations of east Texas. So slavery was allowed even though Mexico had anti-slavery laws.

Kiamata was an Afro-American who helped settle Texas when she was a little girl. She was the slave of Dr. and Mrs. James Long.

If we were able to talk with Kiamata, she might answer our questions so we could learn her story.

Where did your family come from? My parents were brought to America from Africa as slaves.

Where were you born? In this country, on the Long plantation. I lived in Virginia, Louisiana and Texas with Dr. and Mrs. Long, as their slave, from the time I was a child.

What did you do as a slave? I took care of the Long's little daughter, Ann, and helped with the housework. I worked for the Longs all my life. So did my daughter, one of my sons and my granddaughter.

Was it hard? Oh yes. It wasn't easy to be an early settler. We had to do everything for ourselves.

When the Longs went to Texas in 1820, I was with them. We lived in a fort known as Fort Bolivar. Dr. Long was gone for two years on an expedition to Mexico. It was lonesome there, but Mrs. Long would not leave because she thought her husband would return.

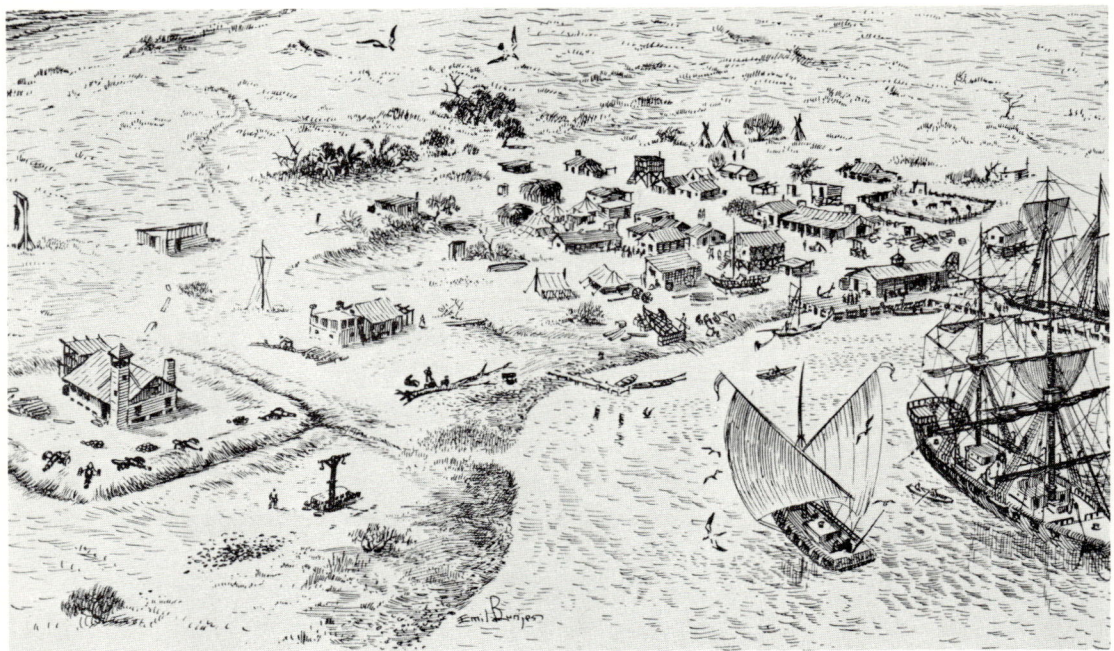
Port of Galveston: 1818

Weren't there other people living in Fort Bolivar?

For awhile, yes. But when time passed and the members of Dr. Long's expedition did not return, everybody, except Mrs. Long, Ann, her daughter who was five years old at the time, and I, left. *Even the soldiers left the fort.* We were alone.

Weren't you afraid?

Sure I was. The weather during those two winters we were in Fort Bolivar was very bad. We were afraid the Karankawa Indians would find out that the soldiers had gone and would attack the fort.

I was only 12 years old then. I would go out of the fort to fish for food in a soldier's uniform to make the Indians think that the fort was still well protected.

I used to help Mrs. Long fire the fort's cannon to keep the Indians thinking that there were more people there than just us three.

Did Dr. Long return?

No. We found out that he had been captured and later killed in Mexico City.

How did you get out of the fort? Some members of Stephen F. Austin's group who came to settle Texas rescued us. We went back to Virginia but later returned to Texas to live with the people who settled Austin's colony.

Were you a slave all your life? I was, and so were my four children. But my grandchildren were free. The Longs were good to me, but when you are a slave, you have no way to advance yourself. I am glad that my grandchildren had opportunities I did not have. One of my grandsons, Henry C. Breed, became a veteran officer on the Houston police force. I am proud of my family.

Kiamata Long's great-grandchildren

Kiamata Long helped to settle Texas because she was a brave and loyal person. Other Afro-Americans helped Texas win its independence from Mexico.

Samuel McCullough at Goliad fighting for Texas independence

1835
Fighters for Texas Independence

When the war for Texas independence began, Mexican troops were sent to try to take cannons from the Texans at Gonzales on October 2, 1835. The Texans defeated them.

The word then went out that the Mexican army was again on the move. Volunteers were called to help in the defense of Texas.

Free black colonists and slaves volunteered to fight side by side with white colonists to help Texas become free of Mexican rule. Samuel McCullough and Hendrick Arnold were Afro-American freedom fighters. They could tell us about war.

Mr. McCullough, what do you remember about the war for Texas independence?	I served as an enlisted member of Captain James Collingsworth's company. I remember when the 47 members of our company marched on Goliad where 100 Mexican troops were stationed.

We knew we were outnumbered, but we wanted to take the Mexican garrison. It was October 9, 1835 — the date of a hard battle between the Mexicans and us.

We won! |
| Were there many casualties? | I was wounded in the shoulder. That wound left me an invalid for a year and a cripple for life.

But I am proud to say that no one else in our company was hit by Mexican fire. We fought a good battle for Texas. |
| What did you do after the war? | When Texas became a republic its new laws ordered free Afro-Americans to leave. |

A free black family at home

I was the child of a white man after whom I was named. I had never been a slave. But because my mother was black, I was considered a free black, and, according to the new laws, I could not stay in Texas.

There I was, wounded in a battle to make Texas an independent republic, and I was being ordered to leave! Besides, my wife was the daughter of a white colonist who came to Texas with Stephen Austin. According to the laws, she could stay in Texas, but I couldn't.

You can imagine how terrible that made me feel. Texas was my home. I had earned the right to live there. I wasn't going to let them force me to leave my home.

What did you do? I sent a petition to the Texas Congress asking to be allowed to remain in the republic with my wife and children. It was hard to wait for an answer.

What was the answer? Congress permitted me to stay. The report said that I was among the first to shed blood in the war for Texas independence. I'm glad that meant as much to the government as it meant to me.

Two months after the battle Samuel McCullough helped win, Texan revolutionary troops invaded San Antonio.

Hendrick Arnold, the son of an Anglo father and black mother, had grown up in San Antonio and took part in that attack. He might tell us some things about the battle if we asked him:

Mr. Arnold, why did the Texans invade San Antonio? It was the capital then, and, if you are in a revolution, you try to capture the capital city. We had a volunteer army of two divisions—about 300 men. I was a scout for the division commanded by Colonel Frances Johnson.

San Antonio de Bexar — 1840

What happened? We assembled outside of town, but my unit at first refused to move.

Why? At the time of the attack, in December of 1835, I was on a hunting trip.

The men in my division wanted me to lead them against the Mexican army which was three times the size of the Texas volunteer army and in a good defensive position in town. My knowledge of San Antonio was absolutely necessary.

Was there a battle? Yes — when I returned on December 5. The Mexican army was holding the Alamo and the central plaza of San Antonio. Instead of attacking along the barricaded streets, we went from room to room of the houses along the plaza, advancing on the enemy's stronghold.

How long did the battle last? Four days!
We fought hard during those four days — like guerrillas, weaving our way in and out of San Antonio houses to surround the Mexicans.

Who won? We did!
The Mexicans raised the white flag of surrender on December 9.

Colonel Johnson, my commander, praised me and my men for our knowledge, fighting ability and bravery. It was a hard battle.

Did you fight any other battles? Yes. I served under the command of my father-in-law, Erastus "Deaf" Smith, a well-respected army scout, during the Battle of San Jacinto. We were spies for the Texas army.

What did you do after the war? I was given land as pay for my army service. I stayed on that land with my wife, even though free blacks were ordered to leave the country after Texas independence. I operated a grist-mill in San Antonio close to Mission San Juan.

Hendrick Arnold at the Siege of Bexar

William Goyens lived about the same time as Samuel McCullough and Hendrick Arnold. He was born in North Carolina in 1794. His father was a free mulatto, and his mother was white. We know that he was in Nacogdoches by 1820, and he spent the rest of his life in this east Texas town.

He worked as a blacksmith, wagon manufacturer, freight hauler, mill owner, land speculator and planter. His blacksmith shop was very successful.

Goyen's blacksmith shop in Nacogdoches

During the war for Texas independence from Mexico, William Goyens was sent by Sam Houston to visit with the Cherokee Indian tribe to try to convince them not to help the invading Mexican forces. Goyens spoke Spanish and Indian languages.

After the revolution he helped the new Republic of Texas keep good relations with the east Texas Indians. He knew how to talk with people and win their confidence.

By buying, selling and trading land, William Goyens became one of the very first rich Texans. This is amazing because the laws of the Texas republic kept black people from owning property.

Somehow, though, he owned lots of land and was able to use what he had to build a fortune. He was not only rich, but he was also well-respected, just as Samuel McCullough and Hendrick Arnold were. They had something else in common: they were free.

Other Afro-Americans were not.

1836 Republic and Early Statehood

Working in the fields

The war for Texas independence did not free people who were slaves. The laws of the new republic made slavery legal because plantation owners wanted slaves to plant and harvest their crops.

Slaves had to work hard without pay. But worst of all, they were thought of as property, not as citizens of the Texas republic. Even though they had been born in Texas and many of the men had fought for Texas independence, Afro-American Texans were not allowed the same rights as white people living in the Texas republic.

Some slaves ran away to Florida and lived among the Seminole Indians there. They intermarried with the

Chief John Horse

Indians. For awhile, they were free. But members of this group were occasionally kidnapped and sold as slaves.

Chief John Horse was the leader of the Negro Seminoles. He led them to Texas where they settled on both sides of the Rio Grande. They lived in Mexico and in south Texas. There they were free people. Descendants of Chief John Horse and his tribe still live in south Texas.

Negro Seminole village

Not all Indians and Afro-Americans got along well, however. Brit Johnson's story is an example of the types of things that make people enemies.

Britton Johnson was known as a sharpshooter and skilled cowhand when Texas was still part of the frontier. If he were alive today, we could ask him about his childhood and the tragedies in his life. He might answer this way:

Where did you grow up? In Texas. I was a slave of the Johnson family. When I was a boy, I played with the son, Allen.

As a grown man I worked on his ranch in west Texas. The ranch was part of a settlement in Young County which was then part of the frontier.

What did you do on the ranch? I worked cattle.
I was a good all-round cowhand. I also learned to become an excellent marksman. Few people could match me with a rifle.

Why did you learn to use guns? On the frontier we had to be prepared for Indian attacks. The Indians often raided settlements, and we had to defend ourselves against them.

Can you tell us about those raids?

Oh yes, especially the one when the Indians kidnapped my wife and three children. Indians would sometimes ride onto a ranch or farmstead to take food or cattle. Sometimes they would try to capture people for slaves or to use in trade.

That's what happened to my family. I couldn't rest knowing that they were captives of the tribe that had killed other people in our settlement. So, my master gave me a horse with permission to go after my wife and children.

Did you find them?

For two years I traveled over west Texas looking for them. I thought I'd never find them.

Luckily, I got to know a tribe of Comanches who respected my sharpshooting. I was able to find out where my wife and children were from that group of Indians. As soon as I knew where to find them, I made my way into the Indian camp and rescued them along with some other captives.

Not long after Brit Johnson had rescued his wife and children, he was driving a freight wagon to Weatherford, Texas, with a couple of friends. A band of 25 Indians — we don't know if they were Kiowas or Comanches — attacked the wagon and killed him. They mutilated his body, probably because they thought he had tricked them into telling him where to find his wife and children. But Brit must have fought to his death. More than a hundred used cartridge shells were found around his body.

The frontier was a place where people had to make do with very little. They had to make lots of things for themselves, but some things, like household utensils, they could buy from craftsmen. So, when John Wilson came to the Texas frontier from Virginia, he started a pottery business to supply the settlers with clay jars and jugs which they had difficulty getting.

He brought his slaves to Seguin with him. Among them were Hiram and James. Both learned the craft of pottery

making from English potters. They made very useful and beautiful pottery.

After the emancipation of slaves Hiram Wilson opened his own pottery-making shop in the town of Capote. His nephew, the son of James Wilson, helped him. The pottery made by the Wilsons was marked "H. Wilson & Co." and sold throughout central and west Texas.

Wilson used clay he found in the Capote hills near Seguin. The tools he used were made of wood. He fired his pottery in kilns built in holes in the ground.

The pottery could only be made between March and September when it was warm because cold makes clay too hard to shape. The potters would collect the clay in winter and store it in large vats. In the spring they would mix the clay with water and knead it until it was the right consistency for molding and firing.

The Wilson pots were known by their handles which looked like inverted horseshoes. If you ever see some old pottery, look for inverted horseshoe handles. If you see them, you will have found a piece of pottery made by an Afro-American Texan craftsman who learned his art as a slave and developed it as a freedman.

Not all slaves could become free by joining Indian tribes. Not all were given as much liberty as Brit Johnson was. Not all were taught a craft like the Wilson potters.

Most yearned for freedom but couldn't find a way out of slavery. Yet they could get together and share their problems with one another—through their church.

The black church grew in Texas as a place of worship and a place where blacks would gather in secrecy to be together. It offered people who were slaves hope of a better life for their children and, maybe, themselves. The spirituals and the gospel songs they sang tell of the Afro-American's hope for freedom.

A baptism

Camp meeting

1861
CIVIL WAR HERO
Milton M. Holland

People in the Northern part of the country began to talk out against slavery. Southern plantation owners defended it. By 1861 the question of which view was right became an issue of the Civil War.

In the South blacks were not permitted in the Confederate army. They were expected to stay at home and grow food for the troops. They also took care of the plantation owner's family. Some slaves were killed trying to protect those families from attacks by the Union army.

In the North Afro-American soldiers were organized in separate units in the army. Many showed great courage and bravery. Milton M. Holland, an Afro-American who was born in Texas, demonstrated outstanding leadership during many battles against Confederate troops.

Milton Holland was born on a small farm near Carthage, Texas. He was a slave, owned by Bird Holland, a man who had been secretary of state for Texas. Milton's last name came from his master as was often the way slave children got their names.

During the Civil War Milton Holland served as a Union soldier. He was the first Afro-American Texan to be awarded the Medal of Honor. If we could talk with him today, he might tell us about himself and his experiences:

How did you get to Ohio?

I was unusual because I was allowed to leave home for school in Ohio.

Why did you join the Union army?

I lived most of my life in Ohio where I was a free black. When the first call for volunteers came from the Union army at the beginning of the Civil War, I volunteered. But I was told that I was too young to be in the army.

How old were you then? I was born in 1844. When the Civil War broke out in 1861, I was 17 years old.

What did you do? I tried to get a job as a civilian in the Quartermaster Corps. I was hired as a servant to Colonel Nelson H. Van Vorhes.

When did you become a soldier? Two years later I was mustered into the Union forces and assigned to the Fifth United States Colored Troops, commanded by General Benjamin F. Butler.

Was your regiment all black? Yes, except for the top officers.
During the Civil War and even later, the army had segregated troops. Black and white men were not permitted to serve together in the same company in the army.

Where did you fight? I fought in the swamps of North Carolina and became first sergeant of Company "C." We fought battles in Virginia too.

How did you win the Medal of Honor? Four years after the Civil War began, my regiment was close to Richmond, Virginia, an important stronghold of the Confederacy. We Union soldiers fought the Confederates all during August and September of 1864. Those were long and hard-fought battles. We had many casualties.

By September 29 all of the commanding officers had been killed or wounded. I took command and led the troops in the Battle of New Market Heights. The men were courageous. Even though many of us were wounded, we kept on fighting, and eventually we won the battle.

I was wounded during that battle, but that did not keep me from leading a charge on Fort Harrison later the same day to help a brigade of white troops get back to the Union lines. I was awarded the Medal of Honor for leadership and bravery.

What was your highest rank?

By the end of the Civil War I was a sergeant major. I had been recommended for promotion to captain by General Butler, my commanding officer. I think I deserved that promotion because I fought so well on many battlefields.

During the Battle of New Market Heights in Virginia, I took command of the forces when all the officers were killed. I also led troops to victory in other battles. For instance, in the winter of 1863 my regiment raided parts of swampy North Carolina, capturing Confederate food and supplies and freeing slaves. A year later we raided Yorktown, Virginia, to liberate Union soldiers who were held prisoner at Libby Prison, a Confederate prisoner-of-war camp. We also helped General Kilpatrick, who had been surrounded by Confederate soldiers when his troops tried to save the Union men who were in Libby Prison.

I was with the James River fleet when it advanced on Richmond. I was ordered to have my men attack the Confederates. We followed the orders immediately, without even landing our boat. My men jumped from the guardrail of the boat and waded through waist-deep water to the point of attack. We captured the rebel flag, the signal station and the officers at the station.

This was the first Union blow at the rebel stronghold in Petersburg. We made it possible for other Union forces to continue the attack and finally to force the Confederates to surrender.

In spite of all these victories, the War Department did not follow General Butler's recommendation for my promotion. At that time Afro-Americans were not permitted to hold a rank higher than that of sergeant major. I could not be a captain because of my race.

John Jefferson, Negro Seminole scout

1866
A TIME OF RECONSTRUCTION
After the Civil War

The Civil War ended in April 1865. On the following June 19th General Gordon Granger came to Galveston to proclaim Texas as part of the United States. At that time he reminded Texans of the Emancipation Proclamation which President Lincoln had signed on January 1, 1863. The slaves in Texas as well as throughout the United States were now free.

For a long time after this the 19th of June was considered a day of celebration by Afro-American Texans. There were parades, barbecues and dances every year on that day.

This day is no longer celebrated as widely because younger generations of Afro-American Texans think of it as a reminder of the years before when their ancestors were slaves and the many years after when Afro-Americans have been denied equal rights and opportunities.

The time after the Civil War was a confused and unhappy time. The freed blacks did not know where to go or what to do. Confederate soldiers were trying to find their families. The state government was disorganized.

The United States Congress ordered the defeated Confederate states to hold constitutional conventions before they could become part of the Union again. Texas began to reform the government with a constitutional convention on June 1, 1868.

There were nine elected black delegates:
  G.T. Ruby,
  W. Johnson,
  J. McWashington,
  Ben O. Watrous,
  C.W. Bryant,
  S. Curtis,
  M. Kendall,
  R. Long and
  Sheppard Mullins.

This was not an easy time for the newly freed slaves. White people in the Southern states felt conquered. They were bitter and angry. They felt the way you might when you are angry with your parents. You cannot strike back at them without getting punished. So, you may take your anger out on a relative or friend. The people in the South who became the target of white hostility towards the federal government were the newly freed Afro-Americans.

Strong Afro-American leaders were needed more than ever. After the Civil War Afro-Americans were permitted to become active in government. Those who entered politics then paved the way for others to follow them.

Black members of the Texas legislature in the late 1800's

Just as Afro-American leaders today speak out for equal rights and opportunities for people, so did Afro-American leaders in Texas during the Reconstruction period just after the Civil War. That was a time when the state was required by the federal government to write a new state constitution and form a new state government in order to reenter the Union.

Although slavery was no longer permitted, the attitudes toward blacks had not changed. They were not thought of as citizens with equal rights. Afro-American leaders had to work hard to get laws passed which would protect the rights of the freed slaves and put an end to segregation.

They were not always successful. Attitudes are hard to change. People still discriminate against other people even though we have a Bill of Rights and laws specifically to protect people from discrimination.

George T. Ruby and Norris Wright Cuney were among the first Afro-American Texans to speak out for the rights of black Americans.

An interview with George T. Ruby might go like this:

How did you get started in politics, Mr. Ruby?

When I moved to Galveston, Texas, I joined the Republican Party and became good friends with Edmund J. Davis who later became governor of the state. That was after I returned from Haiti.

What were you doing in Haiti?

When I was only 20 years old, I became a reporter for a Boston newspaper, *The Pine and Palm*. That paper sent me to Haiti. My assignment was to collect stories about life there for readers of the Boston paper.

I spoke out against slavery and the problems black people were having. I reported how the black people in Haiti lived to give people in this country some idea of what life was like for blacks in other parts of the world.

How did you feel about your work as a reporter? It was interesting, but it didn't help me do what I really wanted to do. After the Civil War ended I felt new hope for black people in the States. So I returned to get involved.

What did you want to do? I wanted to help end discrimination against black Americans and find ways to give black and white people equal opportunity.

What did you do after you returned to the States? I went to New Orleans where I became an elementary school principal and then a school supervisor for the state of Louisiana. I moved to Galveston, Texas, just before the election for the Texas constitutional convention in 1869. As I have told you, I was active in the Republican Party in Texas. I decided to run for election to the Texas constitutional convention, and I won.

Were you able to work for civil rights at the convention? I did, but not all members of the convention thought this was important. Nothing was done about the discrimination problem blacks were having after the Civil War. I was very disappointed with what the convention was doing.

What did you do about that? I resigned from the convention and ran for the Texas Senate as the Galveston representative.

I was elected! In the Senate I had better opportunities to work for equal rights than I had ever had before.

G. T. Ruby speaking from the Senate floor

Galveston Harbor, c. 1870

Why? Galveston was an important port of trade. It also had a large population of Afro-Americans who had been active in business for many years. While I was a representative from Galveston in the Senate, I was able to represent the interests of the business people in that city and other parts of Texas. I introduced bills to help Galveston become an important port and to start a state militia. I worked hard to have those bills passed by the Senate to become laws.

Because the business people wanted these laws and saw that I worked hard to have them passed in the Senate, they supported me when I spoke out for civil rights. The support of these people was particularly important in my campaign for voting rights because at that time many Afro-Americans were not being allowed to vote as free citizens.

There were many cases of violence, bribery and threats against black voters throughout the state which I tried to stop by introducing bills to make it illegal for anyone to keep others from voting.

Although I was not always able to make the other senators act to solve many problems Afro-American Texans had, I did make them pay attention to some. I was recognized as an important black leader in the Texas Senate and in Galveston, the place I represented.

The legislators: Ruby, Burton and Holland

What do you think of as the hardest or unhappiest time of your life?

I think the hardest time for me was when I thought there was no hope for equal rights and opportunities for Afro-Americans in the United States of America.

That was one of my reasons for going to Haiti as a newspaper reporter. Even after I returned to the United States because there seemed to be some hope for freed blacks after the Civil War, it was very hard to influence those who did not understand how important the problems of freed slaves were and how important equal rights are for all people in a democratic country.

When I felt that I could not do much more for my people in the Texas Senate, I went back to New Orleans to continue with my earlier work as a newspaper writer.

George T. Ruby was not the only Afro-American who fought for human rights. Norris Wright Cuney also worked hard for this cause. He might tell us these things about himself and his work if we talked with him today:

Where did you grow up, Mr. Cuney?	I was born near Hempstead, Texas, but I went to school in Pennsylvania and even studied the riverboat trade in New Orleans when I was a young man.
What did you do very well?	Even though I never finished school, I found I could do many things well if I studied. When I decided to enter politics, I studied law. I became a very good public speaker. That skill made it possible for me to speak out about the needs of Afro-Americans.
What types of work have you done?	Most of my work was in politics. These are some of the positions I held: Sergeant-at-arms for the Texas House of Representatives; Member of the Galveston School Board; Federal Customs Inspector for Galveston; Secretary of the Republican State Executive Committee; City Commissioner for Galveston; Republican National Committeeman from Texas; Collector of Customs for Galveston. As Collector of Customs, I held the highest federal position in the state of Texas.

What did you like best about your work in politics?

I enjoyed politics mainly because I was able to work for human rights. I became the leader of the Texas Republican Party. I served as a delegate to the state conventions for 20 years! During that time I brought blacks and whites together to form a strong Republican Party in Texas. That was a successful time for me.

What was most important to you?

I always stood up for what I believed to be right and fair. For instance, in 1888 some black leaders said that black Americans should move to South America to colonize territory there. They thought that would be a way for blacks to get around the civil rights problems they were having, thinking that a new colony of black Americans in South America would give blacks a real chance to start again as free people.

I did not agree with that idea. I thought that black Americans had a right to stay in this country and work for equal rights.

What did you do?

I spoke out strongly against the idea. My statements were printed in the *Dallas Morning News* of February 7, 1888.

> "There is much glory and gain for the colored man here, in the land of his birth and here he should stay and fight his way to the front . . . the Negro is a human being and should be considered from that standpoint if people wish to understand them as a race."

I am proud of my belief in Afro-American rights and of the things I said and did to make people understand that Afro-Americans *are* Americans.

What disappointments did you have?

Well, one time I ran for mayor of Galveston and was defeated.

I had another disappointment a year later when I lost an election for the Texas legislature. But losing those elections did not keep me from becoming an important black political leader in my state.

Norris Wright Cuney died in 1898. He never stopped fighting against segregation, even though the Texas legislature tried to make segregation of Afro-Americans and Anglo-Americans a way of life in the state. Over 3,000 people paid tribute to him after his death.

He is respected and remembered as the most influential Afro-American in Texas during the Reconstruction period.

After the Civil War cattlemen and ranchers moved into west Texas where there was a lot of land for ranching. These new settlers were raided again and again by Indians and outlaws. They had very little protection. So Texas asked the United States government to send troops to west Texas to protect the new settlers.

Some were Afro-American units: the Ninth and Tenth Cavalry and the Twenty-fourth and Twenty-fifth Infantry. These men patrolled a thousand-mile frontier.

They became known as "Buffalo Soldiers." That's what the Indian warriors called them. It may have been the

Escort wagons of the Tenth Cavalry

The Tenth Cavalry in the field

buffalo coats they wore in winter that got them the name. Or, maybe the Indians thought the black soldiers' hair looked like that of the buffalo.

The important thing is that these soldiers were respected as fighting men. The soldiers themselves were proud of the name. The Tenth Cavalry placed the buffalo in its coat of arms. Later the Tenth Cavalry changed from horses to airplanes and is today stationed at Fort Hood.

The Buffalo Soldiers were good fighters. Some were good leaders too. But few Afro-American soldiers were promoted to high rank in the military. Few blacks were trained to become officers in military schools.

1877
WEST POINT GRADUATE
Henry Flipper

Henry Flipper was an exception: He was the first Afro-American to graduate from the United States Military Academy at West Point.

Henry Flipper's parents were slaves in Georgia. He was just a small boy during the Civil War, so he probably did not remember slavery, but he felt discrimination because he was black. He was a proud man who dreamed of being an officer in the army. He might tell us about his dream and his disappointments this way:

Lieutenant Flipper, what did you want most to do?

I wanted to become an army officer. I dreamed of the day when I might wear an officer's uniform.

How did you become a lieutenant?	I went to West Point, the academy for officers in the United States Army. One of the proudest times of my life was being accepted to West Point. An even prouder time for me was when I graduated with the rank of lieutenant.
Where were you stationed after you graduated?	At Fort Sill, Oklahoma, and Fort Davis, Texas. That was in the late 1870's when Indians were still fighting white settlers. Those of us who were stationed at one of those forts were frontier soldiers in many ways. We had to defend the fort and the settlements from Indian attacks.
What other army jobs did you have?	My military career ended only six years after I graduated from West Point.
Why?	I thought I could become a good leader and that I could become a high-ranking officer. But in 1882, five years after I had graduated from West Point, I was dismissed from the army.

I was charged with embezzling Fort Davis funds—taking money that didn't belong to me. Those funds were used to run the fort and, as an officer there, I could decide how to use them. |
| **Did you take the money?** | No. I denied that I ever used that money for anything but fort business. But the charge was made, and a trial was held. I was relieved of all my duties while the investigation took place. My court-martial, a military trial, lasted from October 1881 into the next year. Although I pleaded not guilty to the charges, I was dishonorably discharged from the army. |
| **What did you do then?** | I left Fort Davis to work as an engineer for a mining company in El Paso. I even went to Spain to look through libraries there for information about a copper mine that people had heard of but could not find. It was like detective work. I always enjoyed studying and trying to find answers to questions—especially questions about mining for metals and drilling for oil. |

Fort Davis

Was it hard to get a good job after leaving the army? Not really. I had studied engineering and was fluent in the Spanish language. The mining companies in Texas and other parts of the Southwest as well as Mexico needed an engineer who could speak, read and write Spanish.

Did you enjoy your work? I became known as an outstanding engineer. I spent 37 years working in that field. Later I served the United States government as an interpreter and translator of Spanish.

Henry Flipper died in 1940 at age 84, with his fondest dream unrealized — to wear again the uniform of an American soldier. The army changed his discharge from dishonorable to honorable in 1976, 36 years after his death. His remains, carried by the traditional mule-drawn wagon followed by a riderless horse, were moved from Atlanta's Southview to the Old Magnolia Cemetery, where he was reburied with full military honors.

1879
Education

Before the Civil War most Afro-American children did not go to school. They were taught only what they needed to know to work as slaves. The only schools they could attend were church schools. There weren't enough church schools for everybody, so many black children grew up without learning how to read or write. Sometimes Afro-Americans had to ask friends to teach them to read and write when they were adults.

After the Civil War Afro-American children could go to public school. But these were segregated schools. Which school you attended depended on your race. If you were white, you went to one school. If you were black, you went to another school. Black and white children did not get the same kind of education.

The Afro-American Texan who wanted to go to college had problems because there were no public colleges which black students could attend.

In 1879, fourteen years after the Civil War, the Texas legislature voted to start a "normal school" or teachers' college and made it part of Texas A&M University. It became Prairie View Normal and Industrial College. Prairie View was the only public school of higher learning open to black students in Texas until 1947—82 years after the slaves were freed!

It wasn't until 1950 that Afro-American students were admitted to The University of Texas. This happened because Heman Sweatt was not admitted to The University of Texas School of Law. He took his case to court, and the court ruled in Sweatt's favor, that he had a right to be a student at The University of Texas. After that important Supreme Court decision, other Afro-Americans began attending public universities.

Afro-Americans have had to fight for their right to be treated as equals to Anglo-Americans—
>to get an education,
>to find places to live,
>to ride on public transportation,
>to use public buildings
>and to find jobs.

1888
Trail Riders and Cowboys

During the late 1800's there was a place in the South where blacks were respected as equal to whites—on the cattle ranges and ranches.

The Afro-American cowhand knew what equal opportunity meant because he had it. Busting broncs, branding calves, fighting grass fires and riding cattle trails—these are the things cowboys did. Many cowboys moved cattle from Texas to the first railroads in Kansas.

About 5,000 of those cowhands were black. They worked as wranglers and cooks, ranchers and horsebreakers. They moved herds of about 25,000 head of cattle along the Chisholm, Goodnight-Loving and Western Trails.

The work was long and hard. Often only about 11 men would move the herd. To ride those trails you had to be tough and skilled. Whatever his color, a cowhand had to be good to be part of a trail crew or a ranch. The Afro-American cowboys were respected. They left their mark.

"He'll do to ride the river with."

That's what cowhands said about Daniel Webster Wallace. "He'll do to ride the river with" meant that he was a loyal friend and trusted neighbor.

"80 John's" relatives are ranchers in west Texas. From what they tell us about him, an interview with "80 John" might be like this:

Where did you grow up, Mr. Wallace? I was born in Victoria County, Texas, the year before the Civil War began. My mother, who was a slave, raised me in Texas, my home state.

"80 John" Wallace and neighbors during roundup

Why did you become a cowhand?

From the time I was a little boy, playing with the stick horses my mother made for me, I wanted to be a cowhand.

I dreamed of riding the open range and being part of cattle drives.

How old were you when you started learning to be a cowhand?

I was 15 years old when I got tired of picking cotton and going to school. I left home to ride with some cowboys who let me join them on a cattle drive. I learned to do all the jobs cowboys do by working cattle with experienced cowhands. Then, when I was 17, I got a job working for Clay Mann, a west Texas rancher.

I was a hard worker and became a good cowhand. In no time, I learned a great deal about all aspects of cattle ranching.

How did you get your nickname?

In range days it was important to brand all the calves of cows that belonged to a ranch because the cattle roamed open pastureland. You had to get to the calves while they were still with their mothers. Otherwise, other ranchers might claim the calves for their own herds. We called those calves that got separated from their mothers "dogies." Some ranchers added to their herds of Longhorns all the dogies they could find.

So my job for the Mann Ranch was to get out on the range when the calves were still young and brand them with the Mann brand: 80. The cowhands used to tease me about being "knee-deep" in "80" cattle. It was hard work to go after those calves and brand them. But I did such a good job that I soon became known as "80 John."

How did you become a rancher?

Many cowboys spent their money in saloons and dance halls after they finished the long, hard and dusty cattle drives.

"80 John" (on white horse) with family members

I saved my money.

Clay Mann, my boss, used to put $25 of my $30 a month pay in an account for me. That helped me buy my own herd of Longhorns. I pastured them on the Mann Ranch until I was able to buy land of my own. When I was 25 years old, I had enough money to buy 1280 acres of land near Loraine in Mitchell County, Texas. I started my ranch under the DW brand.

How big did your ranch become? Well, I learned to be a good businessman. I even went back to school when I was a grown man to learn to read and write and do math problems so that I could be a good rancher. With those skills and a good business sense, I was able to enlarge my ranch 12 sections. At 640 acres per section, that's a big ranch.

Did you have a family? While I was at school I met Laura Dee Owens who later became my wife. We had four children. I built a house for my wife and children in Colorado City so that the children could go to school during the week while I lived and worked on the ranch. I also taught my children how to ranch because I wanted them to be able to help keep the ranch going when they grew up.

"80 John's" children did continue the tradition their father started. The Wallace family still raises cattle on the ranch Daniel Webster Wallace started in 1885 — almost 100 years ago!

"I was just supposed to break horses," said Mathew Hooks about his work. That is a very modest statement from a cowhand who was known as one of the best.

Mathew Hooks was a native-born Texan. His parents had been slaves, and though they were free when Mathew was born in 1867, the family was poor. The boy was working when he was only seven or eight years old. He drove a meat wagon for a local butcher. Later he drove a chuck wagon for a nearby ranch while he learned how to be a cowboy.

When did you become a cowboy, Mr. Hooks?

I used to ride a mule named Dynamite. The cowboys on the ranch where I worked always teased me about that mule. When I was 16 a rancher named Morris traded me five ponies for Dynamite. That's when I really became a cowboy because I learned to train those ponies, and soon I was busting broncs too.

How did you get into bronc busting?

I had always been interested in horses. Once, when the cowboys teased me about riding a mule, I challenged them to a race. I rode an old grey horse that nobody expected to beat the horses the experienced cowhands rode. But I won! I had a way with horses. The cowboys I rode with kept putting me on their wild horses—until I could ride them all. I became known as an expert horse trainer and bronc rider.

"Bones" Hooks, 1890

What do you think was one of the best things you ever did?

I'm proud of the fact that I started the first black church in west Texas. To get that church started, I had to import a preacher from Fort Worth and a congregation too! I did it because the church was important to me.

What do you think of as the hardest or unhappiest time of your life?

During my lifetime as a cowhand I was accepted by the cowboys and ranchers as an equal. Then I started a grocery store in east Texas where my relatives lived. Some of the people in that community did not like blacks. I felt the prejudice and left after 18 months. It does not feel good to be told that you're not wanted in a town for any reason. It's worse when the reason is your color.

Mathew Hooks was affectionately known as "Bones" by his cowhand friends. He did many things in his lifetime, but he is best known for his work as a cowhand during the time the Texas cattle ranches and ranges were growing.

He is remembered as a man who loved people. There is a tradition in his honor which he started himself:

The Hooks tradition began when one of "Bones's" best friends, Tommie Clayton, was hurt when his horse fell. "Bones" sent a bouquet of white flowers to his friend, thinking that this would cheer him up and remind him of their happy days together. His friend, however, had died. When the bouquet of flowers was delivered, it was put on his grave. After that time "Bones" gave hundreds of white flowers to the outstanding people he knew. The flower was a symbol of the respect he held for the person.

Mathew "Bones" Hooks died at the age of 83 in 1950. During his funeral service a well-known Amarillo man, John Trolinger, walked down the aisle of Mt. Zion Baptist Church and placed a white flower on his coffin. Hooks and Trolinger had made a pact—whoever was living when the other died should offer a white flower as a symbol of friendship between black and white people.

Bill Pickett was the first Afro-American cowboy to be included in the Cowboy Hall of Fame. He invented bulldogging or steer wrestling. How he did that makes a real "Wild West" story. He might tell it this way:

How did you become a rodeo performer?

One day in 1903 I was rounding up cattle on a ranch in central Texas. An angry cow rushed at my pony. I knew she would gore the pony if I didn't do something fast. In a flash, I leaped from the saddle and grabbed the cow's horns. By sinking my teeth in the animal's soft upper lip, I held her. Then, without using my hands, I threw the cow over. Another cowhand helped me tie her up. That's how I invented the technique of bite-em-lip bulldogging.

I like to wrestle steers. I'd ride my horse alongside the animal, jump off and grab a horn in each hand. I'd twist the horns until the steer's nose was up. Then I'd sink my teeth into the steer's upper lip, throw up my hands to show I wasn't holding on and throw the steer over. I always brought the steer down. Lee Moore, a rancher, saw me throw a steer when I was herding cattle aboard a train to Kansas City. He took me to rodeos where I did my act. It was a big favorite.

Bill Pickett's "bite-em-lip" bulldogging

After I joined the 101 Ranch in Oklahoma, I began performing in the Wild West shows put on by the 101 cowhands. We performed for crowds of people in many places, even in Madison Square Garden in New York City. Opening night in Madison Square Garden was an exciting time for me. The steer I was going to wrestle that night broke loose. The animal rushed for the stands where people were sitting.

People began screaming. I dashed right up after the steer, but I couldn't get on his back. Will Rogers followed me on horseback. He lassoed the steer. That slowed him down so that I could jump on his back. I rode that critter back down the stands into the arena. Then I threw him using my bite-em-lip method of bulldogging. The performance thrilled everyone—especially me!

What was your most dangerous rodeo performance?

I had an exciting and happy life. I bulldogged many Longhorns, elks, buffaloes and even a Mexican fighting bull. I think the most dangerous time I ever had was with the bull.

When I went to Mexico with the 101 Wild West Show, I was challenged to wrestle a fighting bull. The animal was one of the strongest I ever saw. But I thought I could throw him. The owner of the 101 Ranch bet $53,000 that I could hold onto the bull's head for five minutes. The people watching didn't believe that I could do it. They thought I'd surely be gored to death.

The bull tossed me about and slammed me into the walls of the bull-fighting ring. But I hung on for a long time. The crowd was throwing things into the arena. Somebody threw a brick which hit me on the head. I had to let go of the bull. I was a strong and brave cowboy, but that performance was the hardest of my life.

Bill Pickett rode for many years with the 101 cowboys. He was never hurt during his bulldogging acts. When he was an old man, he was trampled by a half-broken horse while rounding up horses for a friend. He stayed alive for 11 days after the accident. When he died his friend said that Bill Pickett was "the greatest sweat and dirt cowhand that ever lived—bar none." Other people thought so too. That's why he's remembered in the National Cowboy Hall of Fame.

1910
Sportsmen

Like their cowboy brothers, Afro-American sportsmen are respected for being tops in their field. Among them are two Texans — one fought great fights, the other played great ball.

Jack Johnson came from Galveston, Texas. He learned to box when he was a young man. He might tell us about his experiences if we spoke with him today.

Mr. Johnson, what do you remember about your very first fight?

I remember being always physically strong and big for my age — 6 feet tall and 195 pounds by the time I was 20 years old. This made it possible for me to do heavy work. In my day it was hard for blacks to get a good education and a white-collar job. So I used my size and strength to work as a freight handler on the Galveston waterfront. You had to be tough for that work.

There were lots of fights on the docks. The first real fight I had happened when I was attacked by a man on a Galveston street. I really wanted to run, but my sister Lucy was with me. She got so mad at the man that she made me want to stay and fight. I did and I won. Later I whipped the biggest bully on the docks. I began to think of myself as a good fighter.

When did you have your first prize fight?

I got started in prize fighting when someone offered me $25 for a four-round fight. I won with a knockout. From then on prize fighting was my life's work.

How did you learn to be a good prize fighter?

In 1901 a friend, Joe Choynski, and I were arrested for boxing. Texas had an anti-boxing law at that time. So we were put in jail. The best thing about this for me was that Joe Choynski gave me boxing lessons while we were in jail — when nobody was looking. The best thing about it for boxers and boxing fans was that when the charges against us were dismissed, boxing got a lot of attention in the newspapers. People began to talk about the anti-boxing law. This made more people think that the law against prize fighting was not a good one. It was repealed. I felt very good about that.

How did you get to be the world's heavyweight champion?

I had fought many fights to get a crack at the heavyweight title. I finally got the chance to box Jack Jefferies in Reno, Nevada, and beat him. The title of heavyweight champion was mine! I defended and kept it for five years.

What do you think of as the hardest fight you ever had?

In 1915 I fought Jess Willard to defend my heavyweight title. That was a hard fight. It lasted 26 rounds! I lost the title to Willard.

Jack Johnson fought 114 professional fights in his lifetime — he lost only seven of them. He had a record of 32 knockouts. That's why he was one of the charter members of the Boxing Hall of Fame.

Rube Foster is remembered as a baseball player and baseball club manager who made it possible for black ball players to move into baseball's big league.

Mr. Foster, what do you like to do most?

Play ball!

What types of work have you done?

When I was in elementary school, I started a baseball team. I quit school in the eighth grade to play ball. I became the "right-handed pitching ace" for the Waco Yellow Jackets. By the time I was 18 I was the manager of that team. I played ball and managed baseball teams all of my life.

What do you think of as the best, happiest or most exciting time you ever had?

I took the Yellow Jackets to Chicago to play against the Giants. I liked Chicago. About a year later I went back to Chicago to join the Giants. I became manager and part owner of that team and also played on it. That's what gave me the chance to have a pitching duel with Mordecai Brown of the Chicago Cubs. The Giants and Cubs played a hard game against one another in 1912. I pitched for all I was worth during that game. Brown was a hard man to beat. But we did it. The Giants won 1-0!

What do you think of as the hardest or unhappiest time of your life?

I think the hardest problem of my life was fighting for the right of black baseball players to play on ball teams with white players. I worked hard to prove that black players are among the best.

When I was invited to Chicago to play with the Giants, I wrote back: "If you play the best clubs in the land, white clubs, as you say, it will be a case of Greek meeting Greek. I fear nobody."

I started the Negro National League to help black players become part of big league baseball. That helped the integration of baseball teams which have white and black players pitching, catching, hitting and fielding side by side. But it took a long time for that to happen—too long!

Chicago American Giants, c. 1912

1910
Musicians and Performers

Making music is an important part of life for everybody. There is music to help us express all types of feelings, and we use music to do just that.

Everybody can make some type of music. Some people have the special talent to compose or perform music. They are the musicians who give us songs and rhythms to hear, play and feel.

Two Afro-American Texans are remembered for their music: Jules Bledsoe and Scott Joplin.

They were different types of musicians. One sang operatic music; the other composed and played ragtime. Each gave something special to all people.

Jules Bledsoe was also an actor. He performed in musical plays and operas in which he had to act as well as sing. Another Afro-American Texan who sang is opera star Zelma George; one who acts is Teresa Graves, the TV personality known as Christie Love.

Showboat is a musical play about life on the Mississippi River. One of the best-known songs from Showboat is "Old Man River." Jules Bledsoe, an Afro-American Texan, might tell us about how he got to sing that song and help make it a hit.

Mr. Bledsoe, how did you become a singer?

When I was five years old, I sang a solo in a church in Waco, Texas, my hometown. That's how I started my singing career.

Did you always want to be a singer?

I didn't think so when I left Texas to go to school in New York. Then I thought I wanted to be a doctor. But I found out that I really didn't like medicine as much as I liked music. So I changed my plans and studied music in Chicago, Paris and Rome.

Jules Bledsoe as Amonasro, in Verdi's Aida

How did you become a star?

My big chance came when I got a lead role in the musical play, *Showboat*. The play had lots of pretty songs. Its story was about life on the Mississippi.

When opening night came I was excited. There I was on a Broadway stage ready to sing the song I had rehearsed over and over—"Old Man River." The play was a smash hit and so was I. "Old Man River" became known as my song.

After that I went to Europe to sing. People all over the world knew about my rich, deep voice. I became a famous singing star. I knew what I wanted to do and kept trying until I made it. Sometimes I thought I wouldn't be a hit as a singer. I didn't always get the chances to sing when I wanted them. But I kept studying and practicing and trying until I got singing roles in opera, musical plays and the movies.

It wasn't always easy to keep trying and hoping, but I did. That's why I was a success.

Like Jules Bledsoe, Zelma George was an operatic star. Her greatest interest, though, was not being a star, but helping people of different cultures work together and understand one another.

She was a scholar too. Zelma George finished college and graduate school. She earned the academic title "Doctor" from New York University.

Dr. George was a member of the United States delegation to the United Nations. In 1961 she received the Dag Hammerskjold Award because she did so much to help people of different nations and backgrounds understand one another.

Another Afro-American Texan who became an outstanding musician is Scott Joplin. He was a composer and the creator of a special type of music that became popular — ragtime.

Mr. Joplin, where were you born?	In Texarkana, on the Texas side. I lived in many parts of the United States, but I am claimed as a native son by Texas.
Why did you become a musician?	Music was important to me from the time I was a child. I sang, played and wrote songs when I was a little boy. When I was only seven years old, I learned to play the piano. Making music is what I did best and enjoyed the most.
What kinds of jobs did you have?	Music was my life. I played and sang in bars and cafes and wrote music. My music is called ragtime.
What is ragtime?	It's music with an off-beat sort of beat. That's why it's called ragtime — the beat has "ragged" edges. It's bouncy and alive. Making it was my life's work.

What do you think of as the best, happiest or most exciting time of your life?

The turning point of my life came in 1899. I was playing in the Maple Leaf Bar in Missouri. I was playing my own tune when a music publisher, John Stark, came in and heard my music. He offered to publish the tune and to pay me royalties. It wasn't often that black songwriters were paid royalties in those days. Usually they were given a lump sum and that was that, but Stark wanted me to get all the money I deserved.

The "Maple Leaf Rag" was published. It was a great success. It sold over a million copies, and that was before there were radios and TVs to play songs for everybody to hear. I made a lot of money with that tune. What a great time it was for me!

What do you think of as the hardest or unhappiest time of your life?

My dream was to write an Afro-American opera about a black girl who did great things. I worked hard on that opera. But I couldn't get it published. I finally paid to get it performed, but no one liked it. I felt that I had failed.

A scene from Treemonisha, *Joplin's opera*

Scott Joplin's ragtime is still played. His opera, Treemonisha, *was recently performed in Houston to an enthusiastic audience. The background music for the movie* The Sting *was written by Joplin. He is another Afro-American Texan who gave us a special gift—his music.*

On the following page you will find a blank Personal History Record form for Teresa Graves. Fill it out with this information to help you get started:

Teresa Graves was born in Houston. She grew up in Los Angeles, California, with her two brothers.

She started acting in high school plays and was also part of a singing group called The Young Americans. After graduating from high school Teresa joined the Doodletown Pipers and sang with the group in many places and on TV.

A good actress and singer, Teresa worked in movies and on TV shows. She got her big chance when she took the role of Christie Love, the policewoman, and became the first black woman to star in an hour-long TV series. When she was asked how she feels about this, she said, "I'm just doing a job, and I want to do the best I can."

Teresa has an excellent memory. She can memorize an entire script after she has read it only once.

Teresa Graves is a devout Christian. She refused to play any scene as Christie Love which showed her taking a human life. She spends her off-hours studying and teaching the principles of her religion.

Name: Teresa Graves

Birthdate:

Where were you born?

What do you do very well?

What kinds of things are important to you?

How did you become a TV actress?

What else would you like to find out about Teresa Graves?
List your questions and find some answers.

War Heroes

In 1941 the United States went to war. World War II is what this war was called because it was the second war that was fought between countries throughout the world. The United States got involved in the war when the Japanese attacked Pearl Harbor on December 7, 1941.

Doris Miller, an Afro-American Texan, was at Pearl Harbor. Like Leonard Harmon, another black sailor, he was a World War II hero.

Name: Doris Miller

Birthdate: 1919

Birthplace: near Waco

On December 7, 1941, at 7:55 a.m., Doris Miller was doing his job in the mess hall of the U.S.S. *West Virginia.* The ship was in the Pacific at the Hawaiian port of Pearl Harbor when the call to battle stations was sounded.

Miller raced to the deck just as the Japanese bombs began to hit. He carried the mortally wounded captain away from the open deck. Then he found an unmanned machine gun. He shot down four enemy planes in the first few minutes. This action earned for Miller the Navy Cross.

In early 1943 Miller was stationed aboard the carrier, *Liscombe Bay,* which was sunk in November of that year. Miller was lost at sea.

A destroyer, the U.S.S. *Miller,* was launched in his honor in 1972. Principal speaker at the ceremonies was Congresswoman Barbara Jordan, another Afro-American Texan.

In the navy Doris Miller was never more than a mess attendant. But that didn't make him any less a hero.

Name: Leonard Harmon

Birthdate: January 21, 1917

Birthplace: Cuero, Texas

Leonard Harmon was also a sailor during World War II. He, too, was a mess attendant. But, like Miller, that assignment aboard ship did not make him any less a hero.

In the early morning of November 13, 1942, the U.S.S. *San Francisco* was under attack by a Japanese fleet in the Solomon Islands. The ship was badly hit. Harmon saw the wounded sailors on deck and began moving them away from the open areas.

He was killed while carrying his wounded shipmates out of the line of fire. He was awarded the Navy Cross after his death for this act of bravery. Later a ship was named for him.

A black Texan by the name of J. Mason Brewer became interested in the folktales of Afro-Americans. When he studied these tales he found that quite a few were originally from Europe, not Africa. Brewer published many books of folklore such as these: The Word on the Brazos, Dog Ghosts *and* Aunt Dicy Tales. *He was called "the best storyteller of Negro folklore in America."*

Political Leaders

There are many Afro-Americans who have been and are important political leaders. Of the Texans, a woman and a man are typical: Barbara Jordan, former Texan representative to the United States Congress, and Oscar N. Du Conge, onetime mayor of Waco.

On the following pages there are blank Personal History Record forms for Barbara Jordan and Oscar Du Conge.

Some information about each is included here for you to use in filling out the forms. As you do, think about what else you'd like to know about each person. Then do some research — find the answers to your questions from people, books, newspapers, magazines, films and wherever else you think to look.

She is a lot of "firsts":
first black to be elected to the Texas legislature since Reconstruction;
first black woman to have been elected to the Texas Senate;
first black woman to serve as governor of a Southern state;
first black to be elected to the United States House of Representatives from Texas.

Barbara Jordan was born in Houston, the youngest of three daughters, on February 21, 1936. Her father was a Baptist minister. The family was poor, but so was everyone else Barbara Jordan knew.

In school Barbara was a good student. She was in the top five percent of her high school graduating class in Houston. She was a straight

"A" student in college. To Barbara Jordan, getting an education was important.

After college Barbara went to Boston University to study law. She practiced law in Houston using her mother's dining room table as her desk. When she had saved some money, she rented a small office to work in.

It was in 1960 that Barbara Jordan decided to get into politics. She ran for office for the first time in 1962. She lost two elections for the Texas House of Representatives. In 1966 she tried again.

She ran for a seat in the Texas Senate. And she won! Barbara Jordan was such a good legislator that many of the bills she introduced were made into law.

She was named outstanding freshman senator during her first year in the Texas Senate. When the state of Texas had the traditional "governor for a day" in 1972, Barbara Jordan was selected to serve as the first black woman governor of Texas.

Her greatest achievement was winning the election for representative to the United States Congress from Texas. That was in 1972. She had dedicated herself to making laws to help the sick, elderly and poor of the country. Barbara Jordan was a very highly respected Congresswomen.

Considering Miss Jordan's success in the field of politics, America was stunned by her decision to remove herself from this arena at the close of the 95th U.S. Congress to become a professor at The University of Texas's Lyndon B. Johnson School of Public Affairs. Says she, ". . . having decided that I had done as much as I could do or desired to do in the Congress, I felt that it was natural to participate in the education of others who I would hope could do better than I . . . ."

Name: Barbara Jordan

Birthdate:

What did you do when you were growing up?

Why did you go to college?

What political offices have you held?

What are the most important things you have done as a congresswoman?

What else would you like to know about Barbara Jordan?
List your questions and find some answers.

Oscar Du Conge was the ninth of 14 children. He was born in New Orleans.
When he was a boy his family was very poor. So when he was only eight years old, he worked cleaning and sweeping the floors of a barber shop.

All his life Du Conge has worked to help all the people. He has been a teacher and social worker. He has started and directed many helpful organizations for the people in his community. These include six neighborhood centers in Waco.

In 1974 Oscar Du Conge was elected mayor of Waco by the City Council, but continued to live in a poor section of town because he felt a part of the people there. He understood the problems poor people have and tried to help solve them. He knew what it was like to be poor.

Du Conge tried to help people help themselves. That was one reason he was mayor of Waco and why he started the neighborhood centers there.

He said, "I do whatever I can with whomever I can and I find it rewarding.
In giving you get.
In loving you are loved.
It's nothing new."

Name: Oscar N. Du Conge

Birthdate:

Where were you born?

Where do you live?

What do you like to do best?

Why did you become mayor of Waco?

What do you feel is the most important part of your job as mayor?

What else would you like to know about Oscar Du Conge?
List your questions and find some answers.

Personal Histories

You have met some people in this book who have done some important things. Their answers to our questions should help you understand something about their lives.

Maybe you want to know more about the people in this book or find out about the personal histories of other people you have heard of or you may know.

Try using the Personal History Record forms with people you know. You might like to interview your mother or father or other members of your family. Then there is the next-door neighbor, your teachers and your classmates. Do you know any Afro-American Texans you can interview?

If you ask people to talk about themselves and their lives, you will be surprised at how much you can learn because each person has something different and exciting to share—like each of the Afro-American Texans in this book.

History is the study of people's lives. And every life is history.

Name: _____

Birthdate: _____

These are some questions to start a personal history interview:

1. Where were you born?

2. Where is your home?

3. Where did your parents and grandparents come from?

4. What did they do for a living?

5. What kinds of things do you like to do?

6. What types of work have you done?

7. What do you think of as the best, happiest or most exciting time you ever had?

8. What do you think of as the hardest or unhappiest time of your life?

Other questions you might ask are:
Who are the people who are most important in your life? Why?
What places have you been?
What was life like in your family and community when you were growing up?
What is it like today?
What special events or celebrations do you remember?
What kinds of things have you done which are important to you?
What do you still want to do?

Make up your own questions to find out more
about the person you are interviewing.
His or her answers to your questions can give you
clues to many more questions you can ask to
complete a Personal History Record.

Name: _____

Birthdate: _____

These are some questions to start a personal history interview:

1. Where were you born?

2. Where is your home?

3. Where did your parents and grandparents come from?

4. What did they do for a living?

5. What kinds of things do you like to do?

6. What types of work have you done?

7. What do you think of as the best, happiest or most exciting time you ever had?

8. What do you think of as the hardest or unhappiest time of your life?

Other questions you might ask are:
Who are the people who are most important in your life? Why?
What places have you been?
What was life like in your family and community when you were growing up?
What is it like today?
What special events or celebrations do you remember?
What kinds of things have you done which are important to you?
What do you still want to do?

Make up your own questions to find out more
about the person you are interviewing.
His or her answers to your questions can give you
clues to many more questions you can ask to
complete a Personal History Record.

INDEX

Arnold, Hendrick 25
Austin, Stephen F. 21, 25
Austin's colony 21
Battle of Goliad 24
Battle of New Market Heights 39, 40
Bledsoe, Jules 73
Breed, Henry C. 21
Brewer, J. Mason 84
Buffalo Soldiers 51
Bulldogging 65
Butler, General Benjamin F. 39, 40, 41
Cabeza de Vaca, Alvar Nuñez 12, 13
Castillo, Alonso del 12, 13
Cavalry
    Ninth 51
    Tenth 51
Civil War 37
Collingsworth, Captain James 24
Cuney, Norris Wright 49
Davis, Edmond J. 45
Dorantes, Andrés 12, 13
Du Conge, Oscar N. 92
Education 57
Emancipation Proclamation 43
Esteban 11
Flipper, Henry O. 53
Fort Harrison 39
Foster, Rube 71
Galveston 46, 47
George, Dr. Zelma 76
Goliad, Battle of 24
Goyens, William 28
Graves, Teresa 79
Harmon, Leonard 83
Holland, Milton M. 37
Hooks, Mathew "Bones" 62
Houston, General Sam 29
Infantry
    Twenty-fourth 51
    Twenty-fifth 51
James River Fleet 40
Jefferies, Jack 70
John Horse, Chief 32
Johnson, Allen 33
Johnson, Brit 33
Johnson, Colonel Frances 25, 27

Johnson, Jack 69
Joplin, Scott 76
Jordan, Barbara 89
Long, Ann 19, 20
Long, Dr. James 19, 20
Long, Jane 19, 20
Long, Kiamata 19
McCullough, Samuel 24
Mann, Clay 60, 62
Mendoza, Antonio de 14, 15
Miller, Doris 81
Narvaez Expedition of 1528 12
Nineteenth of June 43
Niza, Marcos de 15
Petersburg, Attack on 41
Pickett, Bill 65
Prairie View Normal and Industrial College 58
Ruby, G.T. 45
Seminole Indians 31
Seven Cities of Gold 14
Slaves 31
Smith, Erastus "Deaf" 27
Sweatt, Heman 58
Van Vorhes, Colonel Nelson H. 39
Wallace, Daniel Webster ("80 John") 59
West Point 53, 54
Willard, Jess 70
Wilson, Hiram 34
Wilson, James 34
Wilson, John 34
Wilson Potters 35

PHOTO CREDITS

Most prints are from the collection of The University of Texas Institute of Texan Cultures—San Antonio, courtesy of the lenders credited. Credits from left to right are separated by semicolons, and from top to bottom by dashes.

Page 11 Vincent Clarence Scott O'Connor, *A Vision of Morocco* (New York: Doubleday, Page and Co., 1923), page 212.
Page 12 Drawing by José Cisneros, c. 1528. Cleve Hallenbeck, *The Journey of Fray Marcos de Niza* (Dallas: Southern Methodist University Press, 1949); Texas Highway Department.
Page 13 Drawing by John E. Johnson. The Institute of Texan Cultures.
Page 14 Drawing by José Cisneros. Calleros Estate, Mrs. Cleophas Calleros, El Paso.
Page 15 Art by Michael Waters. The Institute of Texan Cultures.
Page 16 Map drawn by Martines, 1578. Original copied by the San Francisco Institute of Historical Cartography.
Page 17 Painting by Bruce Marshall. The Institute of Texan Cultures.
Page 18 Painting by Katie Oliver, Texas Southern University. The Institute of Texan Cultures.
Page 20 Art by Emil Benjes, c. 1818. Rosenberg Library, Galveston.
Page 21 Grant Prater, Galveston.
Page 22 Painting by Kermit Oliver, Texas Southern University. The Institute of Texan Cultures. (Also used on dust jacket.)
Page 23 Painting by Bruce Marshall. The Institute of Texan Cultures.
Page 24 *Harper's Weekly*, February 15, 1879, page 121.
Page 26 Engraving, c. 1840. Homer S. Thrall, *Pictorial History of Texas* (St. Louis: Thompson & Co., 1879).
Page 27 Painting by Kermit Oliver. The Institute of Texan Cultures.
Page 28 Painting by Milton Emanuel. The Institute of Texan Cultures.
Page 30 Art by Bruce Marshall. The Institute of Texan Cultures.
Page 31 *Harper's Weekly*, April 24, 1875, page 344.
Page 32 Painting by Katie Oliver, Texas Southern University. The Institute of Texan Cultures.
Page 33 Art by John E. Johnson. The Institute of Texan Cultures.
Page 35 Art by John E. Johnson. The Institute of Texan Cultures.
Page 36 *Harper's Weekly*, June 27, 1874, page 545 — *Harper's Weekly*, August 10, 1872, page 620.
Page 37 *Harper's Weekly*, August 11, 1860, page 509; *Harper's Weekly*, June 14, 1862, page 372.
Page 38 Art by Bruce Marshall. The Institute of Texan Cultures.
Page 40 *Harper's Weekly*, March 22, 1862, page 196.
Page 42 Mrs. John Jefferson, Del Rio.
Page 44 Gonzales Historical Museum, Gonzales.
Page 45 Art by John E. Johnson. The Institute of Texan Cultures.
Page 46 Art by Milton Emanuel. The Institute of Texan Cultures.
Page 47 Rosenberg Library, Galveston.
Page 48 Galveston Historical Museum, Galveston.
Page 49 Maude Cuney Hare, *Norris Wright Cuney: A Tribune of the Black People* (New York: Crisis Publishing Co., 1913).
Page 51 Department of Defense, Washington, D.C.
Page 52 Mrs. Annie R. Lee, San Antonio.
Page 53 National Archives, Washington, D.C.; KLRN-TV, San Antonio.
Page 55 Ft. Davis Museum, Ft. Davis.

Page 56 *Frank Leslie's Illustrated Newspaper,* July 21, 1883, page 353.
Page 57 *Harper's Weekly,* June 23, 1866, page 392.
Page 58 *Harper's Weekly,* December 15, 1866, page 791.
Page 59 D.W. Wallace Estate, Lorraine.
Page 60 D.W. Wallace Estate, Lorraine.
Page 61 D.W. Wallace Estate, Lorraine.
Page 62 Amarillo Chamber of Commerce, Amarillo.
Page 63 Amarillo Chamber of Commerce, Amarillo.
Page 64 Amarillo Chamber of Commerce, Amarillo.
Page 66 Rodeo Historical Society, National Cowboy Hall of Fame, Oklahoma City.
Page 67 New York Public Library, New York.
Page 68 Dr. W.H. Potts, Dallas.
Page 70 William F. English, Austin.
Page 71 Art by John E. Johnson. The Institute of Texan Cultures.
Page 72 Johnson Publishing Co., Chicago.
Page 74 Naomi Cobb Estate, Waco.
Page 75 Hoblitzelle Collection, Theatre Arts Library, The University of Texas at Austin.
Page 76 United Nations, New York.
Page 77 Larry C. Melton, Sedalio, Missouri.
Page 78 Houston Grand Opera, Houston.
Page 80 ABC-TV Network.
Page 81 Doris Miller YMCA, Waco.
Page 82 Naunita Harmon Carroll, Cuero.
Page 83 Naunita Harmon Carroll, Cuero.
Page 84 Melvin M. Sance Jr., San Antonio.
Page 88 United States Department of the Navy, Norfolk Naval Shipyard, Portsmouth, Virginia.
Page 91 The Institute of Texan Cultures.
Page 92 Oscar N. Du Conge, Waco.

9.95